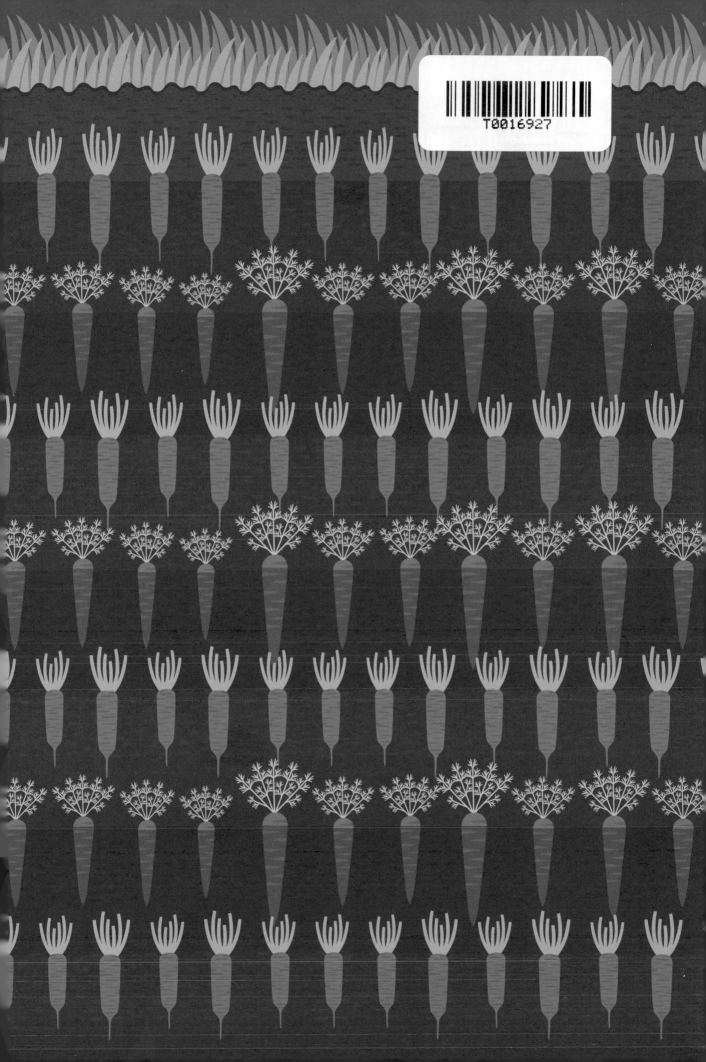

Agnese Baruzzi

FIND ME!
Adventures Underground

Play along to
sharpen your vision
and mind

Wolves ...
UNDER THE GROUND!

Bernard had a problem. He wanted to look scary like all the other wolves. But he had trouble seeing if he didn't wear his glasses. A wolf who could not see well was not a scary wolf. Bernard's pack leader wanted his pack to be the scariest one ever!

No one was afraid of Bernard. He looked so kind with his glasses on. With the help of his glasses and his friends, Bernard was learning see a lot better. He was feeling better about himself, too. He knew his glasses let him see everything. Bernard had used them to find his friends in the forest and the sea.

Life was pretty easy for the wolves. They could hunt anywhere in the forest. Most of the wolves could scare other animals and even people. The leader of the wolf pack was bored though. He wanted to find a new place to explore. He called all the wolves together for a big meeting. "More people and animals need to fear us! We need to visit somewhere new where we can rule," said the leader.

Bernard was worried. The pack leader had come up with some crazy ideas before. It sounded like he was about to think of another one.

"We will go underground!" declared the leader of the wolves.
"There must be lots of things
to find and scare there."

The wolves had to follow the pack leader's orders.
Bernard was upset. "Oh no!" he wailed.
"How will I see underground?
I was just learning to see things in the daylight.
I'll be as blind as a mole. Everyone will make fun of me!"

Then Bernard heard a little voice. "We moles are not
really blind, you know! In our underground world,
we can see just fine. Don't you believe me?
Come with me, and I'll show you!"

The voice belonged to a little black mole.
"My name's Anna. No one knows the underground world
better than I do. Follow my directions carefully and you'll see lots
of things! We'll go through tunnels and below vegetable gardens.
We'll explore dens, caves, and mines. You'll learn so much
about what is underground. And your eyesight will be
better and sharper than ever!
Are you ready?"

Bernard felt a little nervous, but there was no time to answer.
Anna the mole was already heading down.
"Let's go. Keep your eyes open,
and follow me!"

Can you see the queen ant?

Can you find a snail?

Can you see a small skull?

Potatoes and onions grow underground. Three vegetables have buggy visitors. Find them!

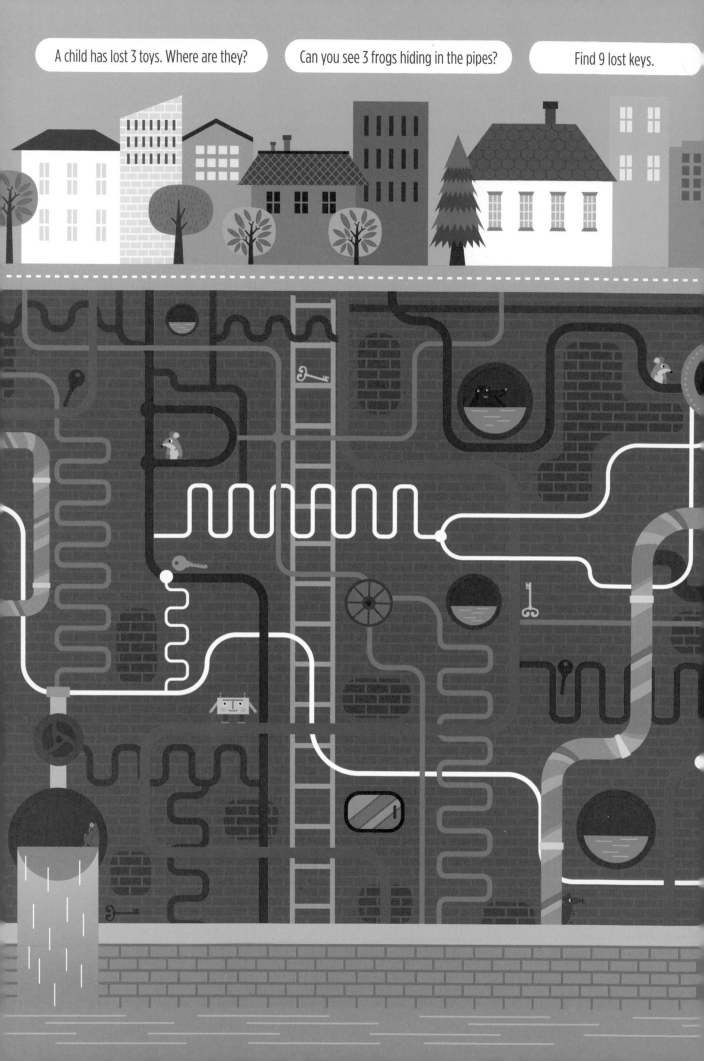

A child has lost 3 toys. Where are they?

Can you see 3 frogs hiding in the pipes?

Find 9 lost keys.

Find 5 ants.

Can you find the squirrel's food?

Find 4 bones.

Each animal on the left page has one difference compared to their "twin" who is sleeping on the right page. Find the 7 differences!

Which bat looks like a pirate?

Can you see an umbrella?

One bat is sad. Which one?

There is an intruder
in the bats' cave.
Can you find him?

Look how many cubs there are in the badgers' den! Only two of them are the same. Help mother badger find the twins.

There is a guest in the rabbits' den. Who is it?

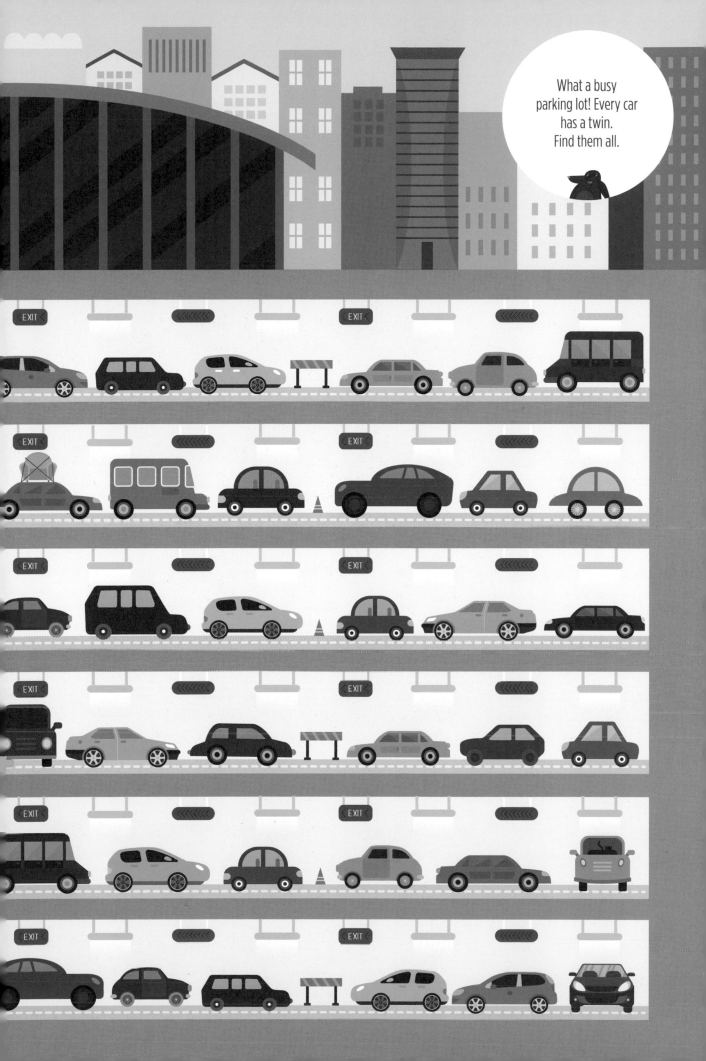

Which skull is weird, and why?

Can you see a prisoner?

Find 3 hidden animals.

Most castles had dungeons to keep prisoners. This one has a kitchen tool in it. Find it!

Can you see a piece of candy?

Who's stealing a precious gem?

Who's hiding in the gold?

There's an object we use for eating hidden in the pirates' treasure. What is it?

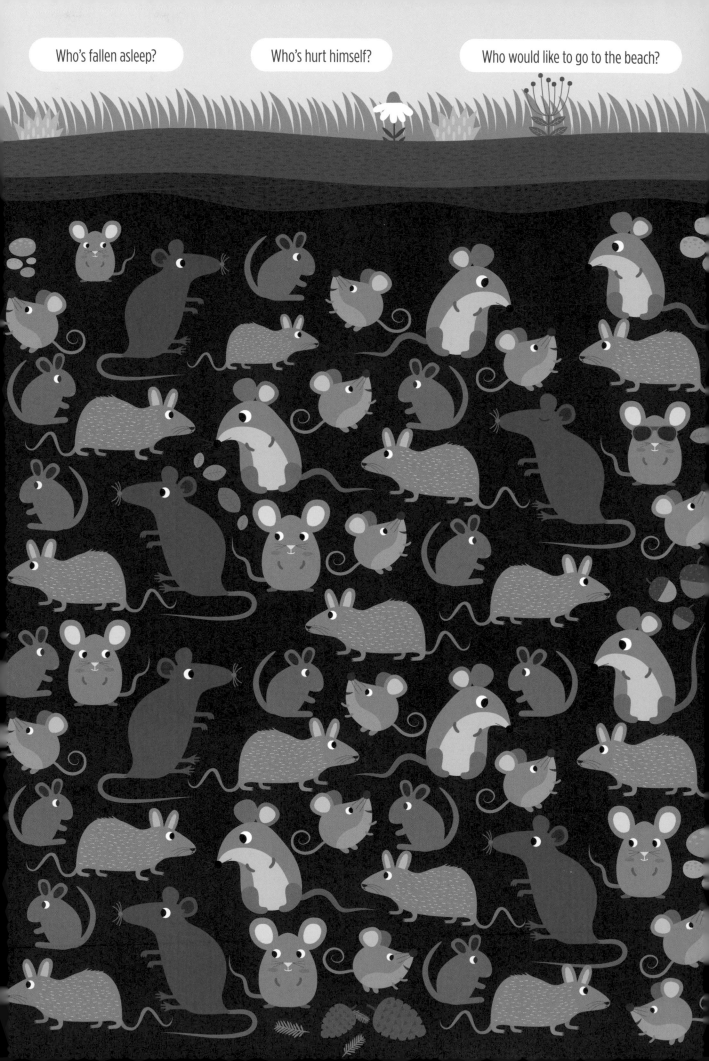

Who's fallen asleep?

Who's hurt himself?

Who would like to go to the beach?

A colony of mice lives underground. One of them is different from all the rest. Find her!

Can you find 8 bats?

Who's having a picnic?

Can you see a broken light?

Three kinds of food are out of place because they don't grow underground. Find them.

Can you find 5 spiders?

Find a teapot . . .

. . . and a teacup!

Each lamp on the right page has a twin on the left page. Find the pairs!

You've rubbed the lamp so hard that two genies have popped out! Find the 10 differences between them.

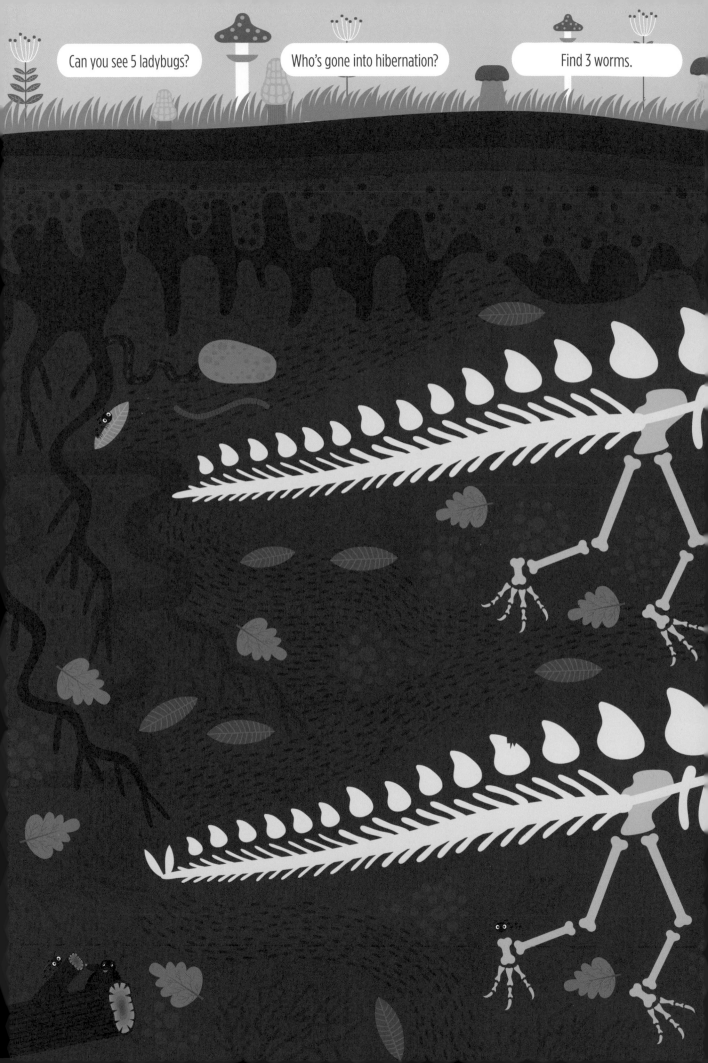

The two dinosaur skeletons look the same, but there are 10 differences. Find them!

Did you correctly answer all the questions?

FIND OUT HERE!

You will find the solutions
to all the games on the next few pages.
Check your powers of observation
and decide if you need to go back
and repeat the exercise!

You will see that some solutions have:

★ A star to show the characters in the main
game and in the special questions.

④ Numbers to help you check whether
you have found all the animal pairs.

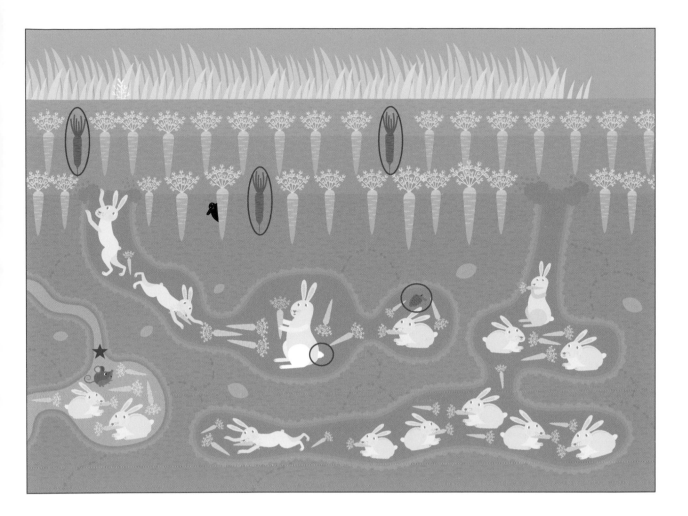
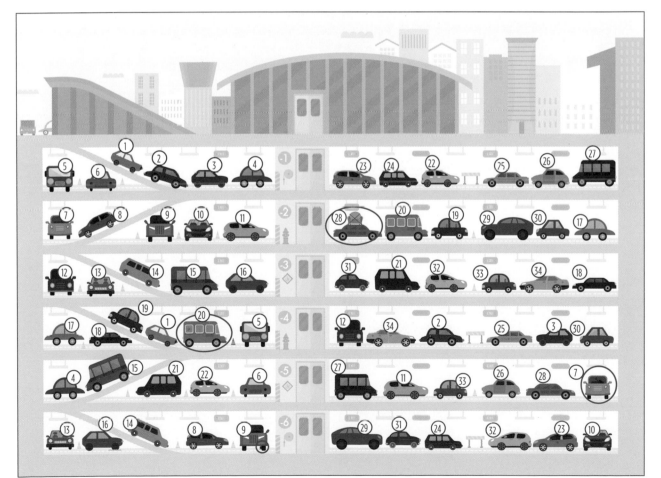

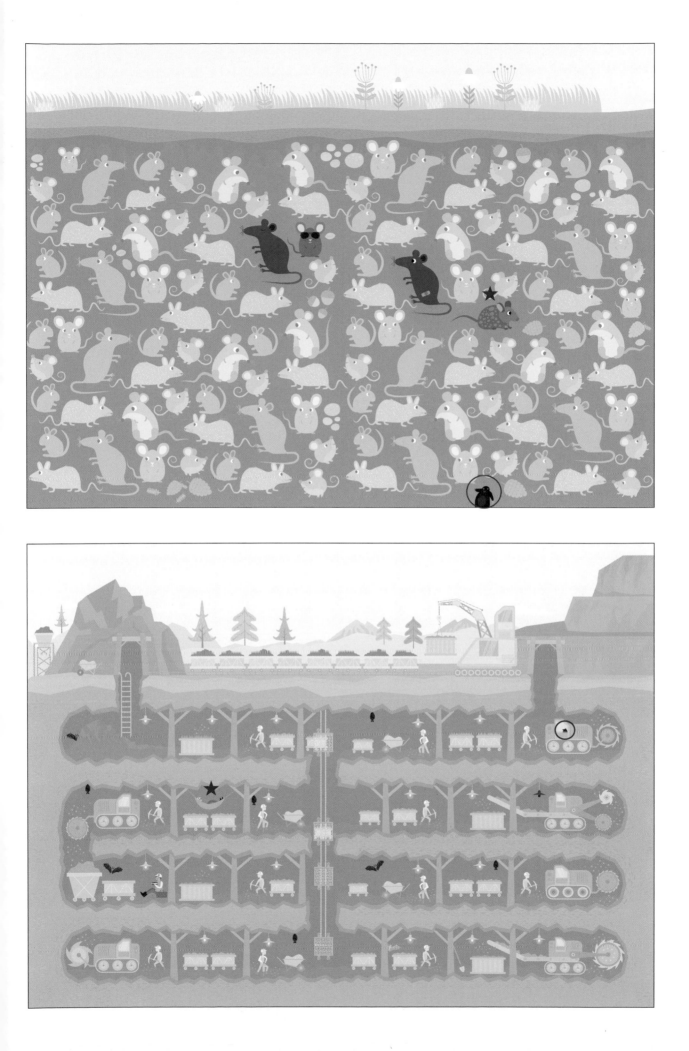

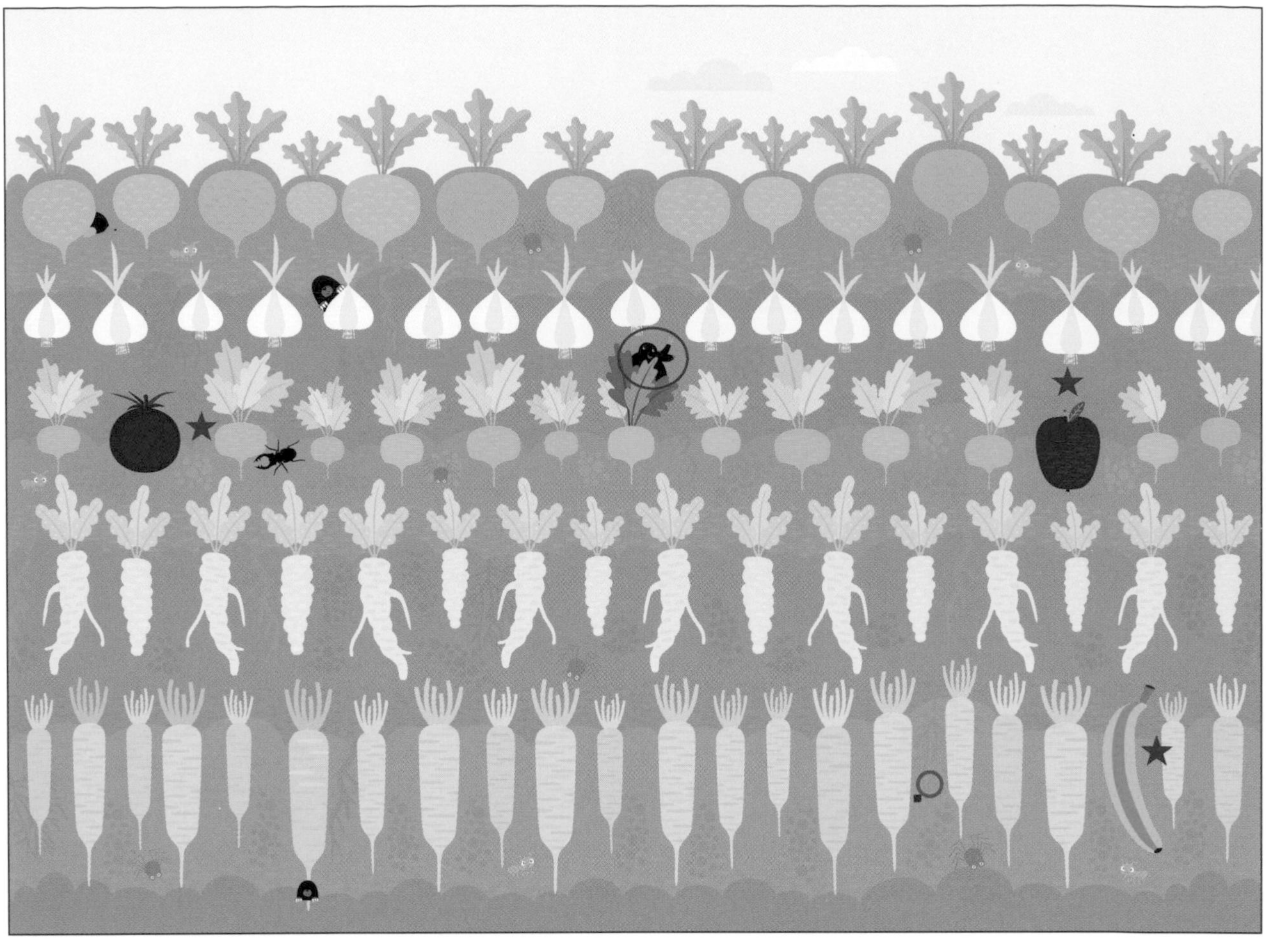

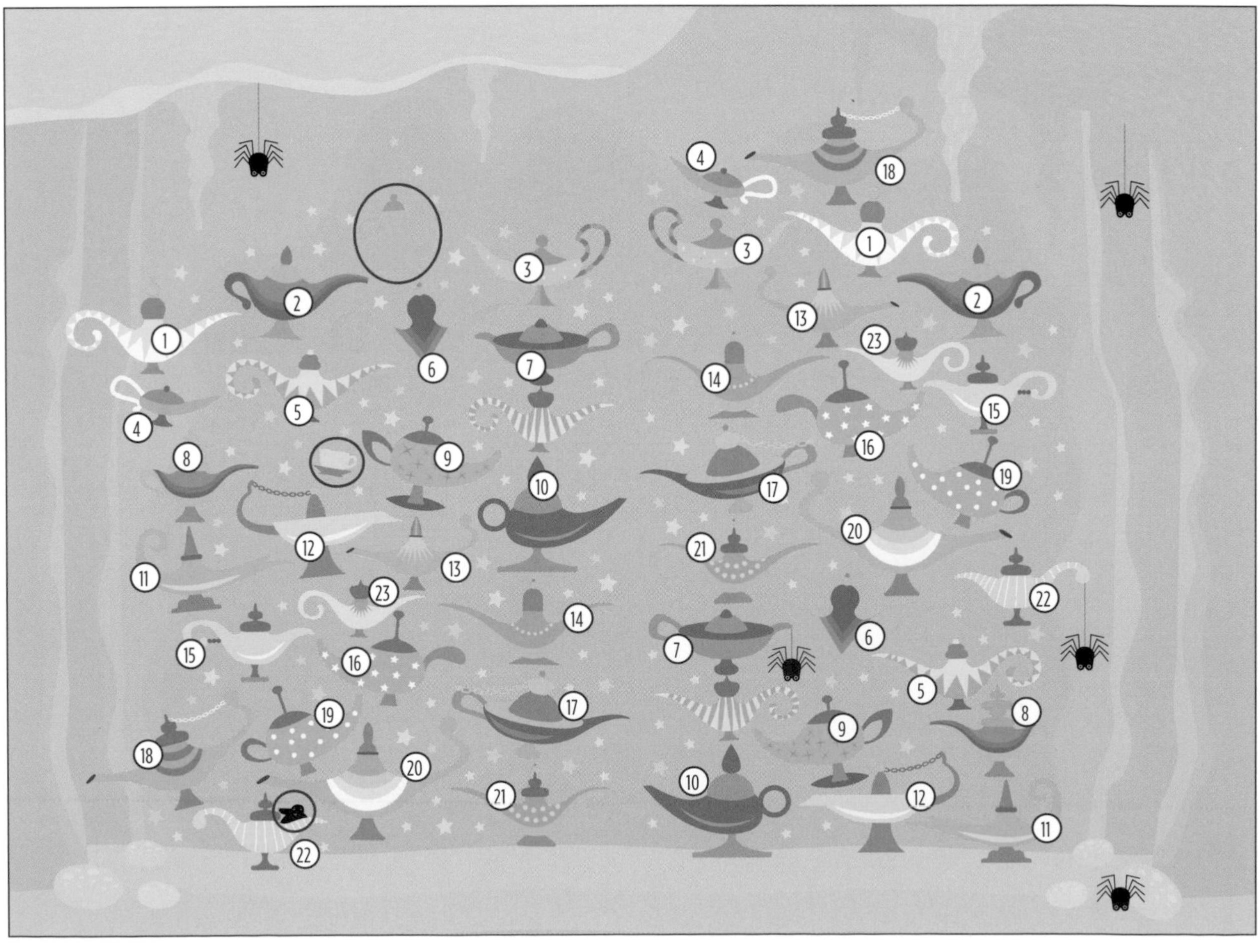

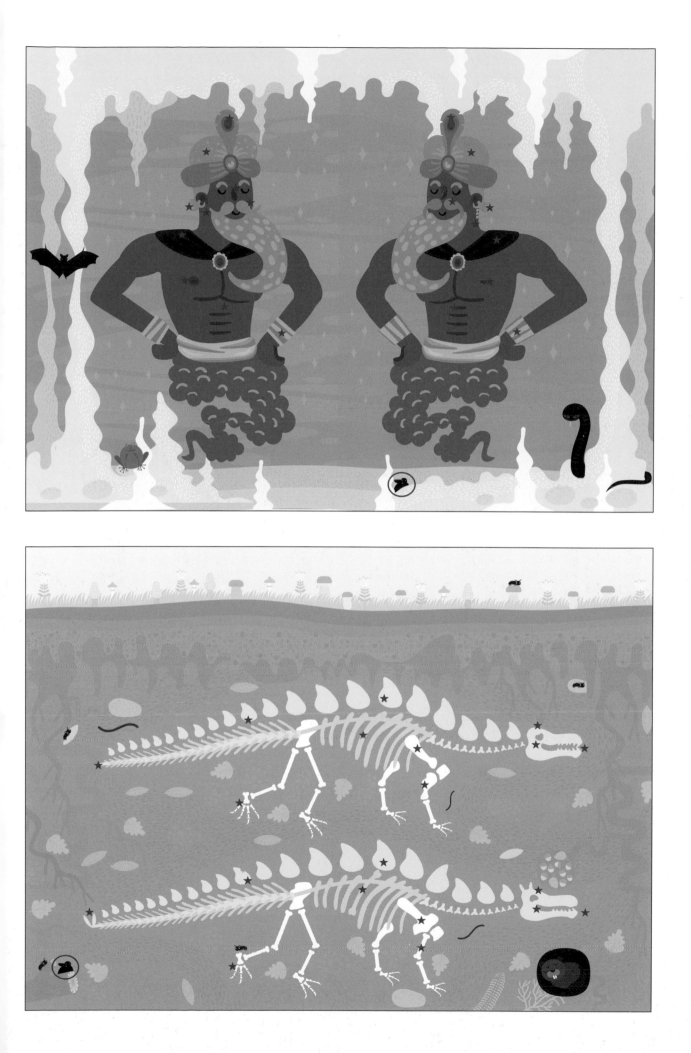

Agnese Baruzzi

Born in 1980, she graduated in Graphic Design from the Institute of Higher Education for the Artistic Industries in Urbino, Italy. She has been working as an illustrator and author of children's books since 2001 in Italy, the United Kingdom, Japan, Portugal, the USA, France, and Korea. She organizes workshops for kids and adults in schools and libraries, and collaborates with agencies, graphic design studios, and publishers. Over the last few years, she has illustrated several books for White Star Kids and Happy Fox Books, including *Find Me! Adventures in the Sky*, *Find Me! Adventures in the Forest*, and *Find Me! Adventures in the Ocean*.

White Star Kids® is a registered trademark property of White Star s.r.l.

© 2020 White Star s.r.l.
Piazzale Luigi Cadorna,
6 20123 Milan, Italy
www.whitestar.it

Translation: TxTradurre, Editing: Phillip Gaskill

Originally published as *Find Me! Underground Adventures with Bernard the Wolf* by White Star, this North American version titled *Find Me! Adventures Underground* is published in 2020 by Fox Chapel Publishing Company, Inc. Reproduction of its contents is strictly prohibited without written permission from the rights holder.

Happy Fox Books is an imprint of Fox Chapel Publishing Company, Inc., www.FoxChapelPublishing.com, 903 Square Street, Mount Joy, PA 17552.

ISBN 978-1-64124-063-5

Library of Congress Control Number: 2020935023

We are always looking for talented authors. To submit an idea, please send a brief inquiry to acquisitions@foxchapelpublishing.com.

Fox Chapel Publishing makes every effort to use environmentally friendly paper for printing.

Printed in China

Fourth printing

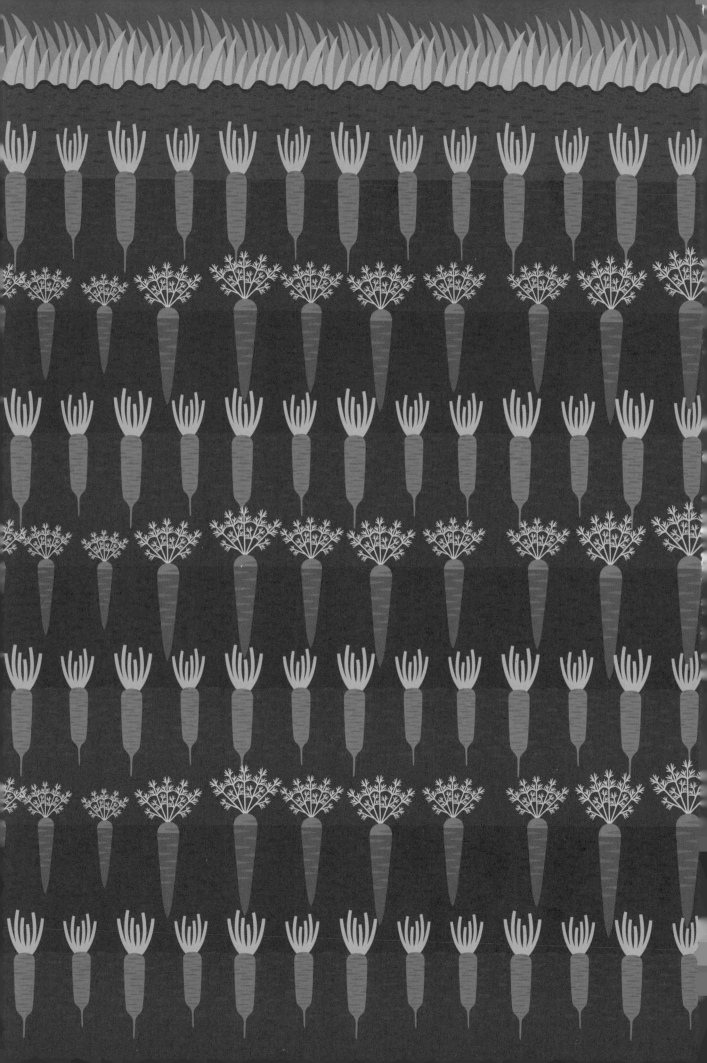